Amazing Manifestation Strategies
- Book #4

THE MANIFESTATION REVELATION

How to Align with Your Higher Self to Manifest Balance, Prosperity, and Happiness

FORBES ROBBINS BLAIR

Forbes Robbins Blair

New Creations Publishing
Gaithersburg, Maryland

This publication is designed to provide accurate and authoritative information regarding the subject matter covered. It is sold with the understanding that the publisher is not engaged in rendering legal, accounting, psychological or other professional service. If expert assistance is required, seek the services of a competent professional person.

—From a Declaration of Principles Jointly Adopted by a Committee of the American Bar Association and a Committee of Publishers and Associations

www.forbesrobbinsblair.com

The Manifestation Revelation / Forbes Robbins Blair —1st ed.

4th book from the Amazing Manifestation Strategies series.

Contents

Why the Higher Self Matters?

IT IS NOT JUST THE DESIRE for status, success, security, or sex that drives us. Because when many people achieve those things, frequently they are still not satisfied. I have found that achieving your most cherished desires comes when you get to that buried and unknown part of yourself.

In the western mystery tradition of wisdom, it is not about acquiring the most precious material treasures: it is about mastering yourself so you can also master the phenomenal world. You do not hide away in some cave and sit at the feet of a guru who enlightens you. That is not the western path. You must journey along with determination and patience until you understand yourself and the outer world, and until you discover what you truly desire and how to get it.

The treasure you will find can be called the essence, the water of life, or the breaths of Gods which are all just different terms for the radical change that you will need to achieve. It means you need to turn doubt, hatred, emptiness, fear, and insecurity into what is positively possible for you in the Universe. And you can only do that with your Higher Self to guide you because if you do not understand your Higher Self you will not be able to answer what you deeply desire. In fact, you won't even be able to ask the right questions. This book will help you find those questions and will even answer some of them.

Understanding your Higher Self can give you that wisdom to understand the deepest questions in Life, the hidden dimensions of your consciousness, in fact of *all* consciousness.

I have found that there is no way to achieve this knowledge except through direct, conscious application of the correct strategies over a long period. I am more advanced at this than when I started over two decades ago, but I am still learning. Indeed, I am far happier and more comfortable with my place in life now.

The good news is that you do not have to have total understanding of your Higher Self to align with it. As you learn to align, the things you want will become clearer and within your grasp.

Your Higher Self has stunning revelations waiting to be opened, even if you might want to discount them now. When you embrace what it reveals— without struggle, without separation and without resistance—you will experience more wholeness and more abiding purpose. You will embrace the idea of manifesting the best in life with your older, wiser Self. Then, your inner voice will say: "Ah, I am really feeling good about this." And you will experience life contentedly, and with exuberance and quiet joy.

In our fast-paced world of textings and tweetings, we have forgotten to search, develop, and trust the ever-available wisdom of the Higher Self. This book will, first, help you see the mystery of what the Higher Self is. Second, it will inspire you to do the work to get the most from it. It will not be hard work, but it will require your attention and some consistency.

The Higher Self, and what it means to the subject of manifestation, is incredibly real and profound. It will envelop you with a powerful confidence that you are truly a part of what existed, what exists and what will exist.

As you come to discover this wisdom, you will have moments of wonderful, concentrated isolations where all else surrounding you will blur and recede while you become aware of your Higher Self, as well as who and what you really are. These startling, "flash realizations" will often seem very powerful and life-changing, and they may come when you least expect them, perhaps during or after you have read this book.

My goal here is to help you recognize what your Higher Self is asking of you, to know when you are pursuing the correct path toward alignment, and to apply what you will learn to your desires in the real world. For the spiritual and the material are not opposites as some people think: they are but two sides of the same, working together.

"That which is above is as that which is below. And that which is below is as that which is above for the performance of the miracles of the One Thing."

—from the Emerald Tablet of Hermes

Was it not the character Sherlock Holmes who said you need to begin your search for answers to the questions of life with this: something unknown wants to be known? The Higher Self has mysterious secrets that can be revealed quickly if you know where to look. And this book is a great place to start.

Manifestation and Your Secret Ally

YOU AND I LIVE IN A SEA OF living, mental energy. And we use the power of thought to shape our reality and life circumstances. We do that by focusing our conscious and subconscious thoughts on what we want because this automatically attracts opportunities to bring our desires into our real lives, into manifestation.

It is a glorious power we all possess and use constantly, whether we know it or not. The aim of each volume in my Amazing Manifestation Strategies series of books is to add to your knowledge about your natural creative abilities to use your manifestation power more wisely to get what you want as quickly as possible.

And while it is good that there are specific things you might want to manifest, wouldn't you agree that balanced prosperity is a key to a happy and fulfilled life? After all, what good is having billions of dollars if you lack compassion and charity? What good is climbing to the top of your career ladder if your relationships are falling apart? What good is being famous and well-respected if you are too busy to enjoy it or your health is failing?

So, perhaps the goal should not be to simply manifest successfully in one area of life, but to manifest well in all of them. That is where many of us run into serious trouble.

Manifestation is like a juggling act: you can throw and catch one ball in the air easily enough, but can you manage to juggle the others at the same time?

Without a more complete understanding of manifestation and its laws, your efforts might bring forth unforeseen consequences you never intended. You might even start to believe that a Trickster runs the Universe. I know a man who used his mind power to attract money so he could retire early and comfortably. So, each day he would work on this by simply picturing himself with mounds of cash in his hands. He was surprised that he ended up working as a bank teller. Lots of cash to handle, true; only none of it was his.

Imagine if someone with wonderful manifesting knowledge could help you. Wouldn't it help to have a friend who would provide the guidance you need to manifest a balanced and prosperous life? There is no need to imagine it because you already have such an ally: it is your Higher Self. Now is the moment to recognize this, and to align with that powerful, knowledgeable friend.

In this book, you will learn more about your incredible ally, about who and what your Higher Self really is, and about how ready and able it is to help you manifest a better life.

By cooperating with your Higher Self, you will succeed at manifesting what you truly want. Surprisingly, you can often do it easily.

Why I Wrote This Book

THE MISSION OF THIS BOOK is to provide you with workable strategies to align your manifestation efforts with your incredible Higher Self.

To align your manifestation efforts with your Higher Self is by far the most important component of manifesting. Without it, those efforts could lead to misery.

I recently received an email from an Irish reader of the first three books in this series. He enjoyed them, and recognized I possess a deep and practical knowledge of manifestation, where I explain the complex concepts in a simple, down-to-earth way. He urged me to focus my next book on the Higher Self as it relates to manifestation. Toward the end of the email, he touched me deeply by saying how afraid he felt about his future and the world's.

I have received many other emails like his asking me to tackle this subject too.

Why I Hesitated to Write About the Higher Self

I hesitated to take on this subject for a long time because it is controversial for people of different religious faiths. I certainly did not want angry people writing me to say, "What about Jesus!?" for example.

I finally asked my Higher Self aloud, "Is this something you want me to write about?" I did not meditate about it. There were no sudden flashes or grand revelations. No angel appeared saying, "Yes, Forbes, you must write that book to save humanity." Happily, I have gotten past the stage of needing fantastic metaphysical or "supernatural" events to affirm my decisions. If it was something my Higher Self wanted, then I would feel compelled to write about it. I knew the urge would persist despite any reservations, and it did. So here we are.

This book contains some of my ideas and recommendations about aligning with the Higher Self based on what I have learned and practiced so far in my life.

I have been actively working with the Higher Self as it relates to manifestation since the early 1990s.

Why This Book Is for You

THIS BOOK IS FOR YOU if you already understand that you possess the ability to manifest and you want to do it more powerfully, harmoniously, and abundantly. It's for you if you want to manifest things that truly benefit you physically, psychologically, and spiritually.

I do not promise that you will instantly "manifest your millions" or become famous or fabulously successful at everything. Perhaps those things will happen for you, but that is between you and your Higher Self to determine. However, when you align with your Higher Self powerfully and correctly, you will be very pleased with what you can manifest.

It will make you happier than you are now, and you will become more successful than you have ever been, and prosperous in ways you have not yet imagined.

If you have not yet recognized the existence of your manifestation ability, then I suggest you put this book aside for now and read my first book in this series, *The Manifestation Manifesto*.

Also, this book might not be for you if you refuse to consider the possibility of the Higher Self. I will not spend chapters to convince arrogant, cynical skeptics who won't allow themselves to discover things outside of the scientific method. Often, they only trust things that can be seen, touched, or measured. This book is for those who want to reach higher.

Here is what I hope you will do as you read further. Concentrate, filter it through your own experiences and beliefs, and then decide whether the information and strategies here are worthwhile. In other words, if it speaks to you keep it. If it doesn't, let it go.

If you have read any of my other books, you know I am all about practical applications. The information and strategies within these pages will help you gain awareness of your Higher Self to manifest the good things you want in life.

With persistence of effort, you will
come to realize your Higher Self is real.
This will lead you to achieve a higher
level of manifestation power.

By integrating your Higher Self in the best way, you will be successful most of the time with less effort.

What is the Higher Self?

A LOT OF PEOPLE TALK ABOUT the "Higher Self," but it is often unclear what they mean when they use that term. For a long time, it was confusing to me also. There are so many books and teachers using the term, and the definitions get muddled to the point where it feels like we are left with a bunch of spiritual or metaphysical gobbledygook. I want to define what I mean by the term Higher Self.

> *Your Higher Self is the <u>real</u> you. It is <u>not</u> your personality. For practical purposes, it should be considered another Being altogether because it is so different from how you conceptualize yourself.*

The first time I heard about this was when I first studied Hawaiian metaphysics (called *Huna*) in the early 1990s. I turned to Huna because I was assured its teachings would not contradict my religious beliefs. This was important to me, as I was just starting to transition away from my fundamentalist Christian mindset.

I suspected there was more to reality than evangelical Christianity revealed. I thought Huna would allow me to safely learn about metaphysics while I could expand my awareness of the spiritual landscape without violating my religious convictions. And I was right.

Huna teaches there are three aspects of the Self: Lower, Middle and High Selves. The Lower Self corresponds to what most of us call the subconscious mind. The Middle Self refers to the conscious mind. The High Self refers to what the *kahunas* (Hawaiian holy men) called the *Aumakua* (the utterly trustworthy parental spirit).

Huna also reveals that the High Self is already part of each of us, and is always available to lend support to our endeavors. I learned that help from High Self may be sought to meet goals and manifest intentions. I worked the techniques I was taught and got impressive results. But that was only a beginning.

Over the years, I have discovered the Higher Self-concept is found in many spiritual traditions by different names. It is sometimes called Vishnu, the Logos, Adonai, the Silent Watcher, the God Within, Yechidah, the Holy Guardian Angel, and many other names.

*No matter what you call it, it is
essential to recognize that the Higher
Self is NOT a human mental construct.
It is not a product of the imagination.*

It is not some vague, abstract, or idealized part of your personality. It is not your kindness or generosity or virtuous qualities. The Higher Self is real. It exists whether you realize it or not.

Your Higher Self is the true power and presence behind your personality (or *above* it to be more accurate). You are its vessel, its vehicle and the object of its purpose and affection. You are like a car and the Higher Self is the driver. You are like a computer and your Higher Self is the end user.

It reminds me of the movie *Tron*. Remember that movie? The character Flynn, played by Jeff Bridges, gets sucked into a virtual world where the people he meets appear to be autonomous but are functions of the computer. Watching that movie may reveal more about the relationship between you and your Higher Self. There are a lot of pop culture references to the relationship between the personality and the Higher Self if you look for them. That is why I reference them here.

If the Higher Self is Real, Why Don't You Experience It?

You may wonder if all of this is true, why does your Higher Self appear to be so coy about its existence? Why hasn't it made itself clearly known to you? It is the same argument atheists make about the existence of the Divine. They ask, "If God is real, why doesn't He just make it obvious and clear?" I wondered this for a long time too.

However, in 2002 I had a vision. Yes, an actual vision. Some might say it was just a dream because it took place while I was "asleep," but it had a different quality to it. I knew immediately this was something unique.

In the vision, I saw a simple bar graph that showed the evolutionary progress of humanity and how we had not even reached one third of our eventual destiny as a species. Not even a third! In my vision, I thought that it was false how we imagined we were so advanced when we were still so immature to the Universe.

Most people on the planet have not yet reached the levels of awareness necessary to be consciously aware of their Higher Self, and that is why they do not have any direct knowledge or perception of It.

All human beings have an entire set of dormant supersensory powers which only a few have awakened. These powers go beyond the scope of contemporary scientific instruments and reveal a complex, multi-planed Universe that gives us direct perceptions of things labeled as metaphysical, spiritual, or supernatural.

As these powers unfold, perhaps the biggest revelation that occurs is that everything in the Universe is *alive*. Do you believe that the sun in the sky is just a big ball of gas and fire? Or that the rocks beneath your feet are just a collection of inert carbon matter? Or that a river is nothing but flowing H20? They possess consciousness! And anything that has consciousness can be influenced by other things with consciousness. That is manifestation at work.

It is crucial to develop awareness and rapport with your Higher Self, because it already knows all of this. It has abilities to manifest magnificent things through you with its vast knowledge and resources.

Eventually, we will all have direct knowledge and communication with our Higher Selves. By the word "eventually," I do not necessarily mean in your lifetime. Your existence did not begin when you came into this life, and it will not end when you transition out of it. But when we finally perfectly align with the Higher Self, we will be able to manifest a world of peace, beauty, and incredible abundance.

That is because your Higher Self is your connection with the Divine. It can directly understand what people call *God*, and present that information to you for your highest good and greatest prosperity.

You might think life would be a lot easier if the Higher Self would instantly change you to live abundantly and harmoniously right now. But as far as I can tell, that is not the way evolving consciousness works. You are an unfinished expression of your Higher Self. You are a work in progress. So, to create something, there must be a sense of separation, of being apart from the one who designs it. This process is known as *involution.*

> *"Involution" creates a partition in your mind that generates the illusion you are separate from your Higher Self. This explains why you have felt lost, alone and aimless at times. But when you can see through the appearance of separation and are no longer fooled by it, you realize your Higher Self is with you—now and always.*

Your next questions may be about how and when you will be able to see through that illusion and become aware of your Higher Self. I cannot say precisely, but what I can say with confidence is that your journey has already begun! You are on your way and farther along than you might think because your Higher Self has been guiding you toward this revelation for a long time. If you look carefully at your life, you will find evidence of that in the most peculiar places probably starting in your childhood.

Here is one example from my own life. When I was about 12 years old in the late 1970s, there was a Top 40 song by the Bee Gees' younger brother, Andy Gibb, called "An Everlasting Love." There was something I really liked about it, so I bought the 45rpm and listened to it over and over (like kids often do) in my parents' basement until the song was a part of me. I remember my father calling down, imploring me to play some other song because he could not stand to hear it another thousand times. Anyway, back then I thought it was a light, bouncy tune that just made me happy.

However today, I recognize that the lyrics to "An Everlasting Love" are unmistakably written from the perspective of the Higher Self. Lyrics like: *"I have been here all your life watching your crying game,"* and *"I was yours before the stars were born and you were mine,"* make the composers' intentions clear. The song tells much about the sense of separation, the pain it produces and the peace and joy when realization and alignment finally occur. Also, my interpretation of that song is not simply due to bias because the same composers released other songs with a similar theme. They obviously knew about the Higher Self, and were gently and cleverly alluding to it through a seemingly simple pop song.

Years later, when I discovered the meaning of "An Everlasting Love," tears came to my eyes because I knew my Higher Self had arranged for me to hear and enjoy that song when I was a kid. A seed had been planted in my subconscious that would germinate to help me eventually gain awareness and understanding of my Higher Self.

Your Higher Self has been doing similar things for you all *your* life. It has been subtly communicating with you for many years in a variety of ways. If you search your past carefully, you will discover this too. For example, say you thought your interest in this book and subject was *your* own idea. Think again. Those seeded events that led to this moment were planted years ago, and perhaps you have only recently been able to understand and respond to them. You probably wouldn't have been able to comprehend them back then. But now you can, and your life is about to get a whole lot more interesting.

What Your Higher Self Wants and Why It Matters

Your Higher Self guides you through a long series of experiences, with many joys and sorrows to produce a magnificent, unique individual with the perspectives and capabilities no one in the Universe can precisely duplicate. Conflicts and difficulties are part of the process, and are necessary.

Like a diamond, you are placed under enormous pressures in life. Like a piece of steel which is being shaped and tempered by the blacksmith, you will eventually become stronger and sharper. Each tempering process can be slow and even painful, but the masterpiece will be forged.

So, what does your Higher Self want for you?

Your Higher Self wants you to live the most happy and productive life possible as you mature at this stage of your development.

By "happy," I do not mean that your Higher Self wants you to have endless financial resources or become instantly successful at everything. Happiness can be found even if you are poor or struggling. Even if you are experiencing pain. Do you think happiness is the sole province of the rich and healthy? I assure you it is not.

David W. Underwood, a compassionate and generous friend of mine, recently told me that he used to be, in his words, "an a**hole." I did not believe him, and I thought he was just exaggerating. He said he had been so arrogant and awful to people that his mother arranged an intervention with his family and friends where they sat him down and told him how insufferable he was and how he needed to change. But it didn't work.

David revealed it was only after he was diagnosed with lymphoma, endured treatment, and came through it healthy again that the ice around his heart melted. He emerged the loving, caring individual he is today. To me, it is obvious that his Higher Self guided him through that troubling experience for a deeper purpose.

And when I say that your Higher Self wants you to be productive, I do not necessarily mean for a career, a job, or some pet project. Some people who outwardly produce very little or whose lives appear the messiest may be the most productive of all when it comes to inner development and progress. That is why we should never judge anyone by some outward standard we believe they should demonstrate. Since their relationship with their Higher Self is different from yours, you and I never know what stage of development that person is undergoing. Comparisons are unfair. What may look bad from your perspective may be necessary for them now.

This is also why you should never judge yourself when you wrestle with your imperfections or problems. Just know that eventually you will triumph. When it comes to your dark times, remember this saying attributed to Sufi poets: "And this, too, shall pass."

As for what your Higher Self wants *from* you:

When you are capable of it, the Higher Self wants you to become aware of its presence, to align your will and desires with its own, and to increasingly identify with it. It wants you to consciously participate in your progress.

This may sound like some sort of call to moral or religious obedience, but that is not what we are talking about. Remember that your Higher Self is your REAL Self, and any separation is only an appearance, an illusion.

However, that illusion often tricks us. Instead of looking to our Higher Self for guidance to determine who we are, what we want and what we do, we often look at the outer world to form our identities. This need to identify ourselves comes from somewhere deep within. It is there to make us search for the answers. The singer-composer Gary Wright, best known for the classic tune "Dream Weaver," recorded a haunting song called "Who Am I" which expresses this longing: "*Who am I? Where am I?*

Where am I coming from?" Perhaps you can relate to it.

Starting at birth, we are influenced by our parents, our religions, our society, peers, teachers, scientists, psychologists, and the media to inform us who we are, what we want, and what our lives should look like. We create a false sense of identity, called the *false ego,* which we mistake for the True Self. It so hypnotizes us we feed, serve, and defend it, even when it makes us miserable or when we know it is not right for us.

In Robert Anton Wilson's mind-rattling book, *Prometheus Rising,* he shows how our brain circuitries trap us while our inner programming shapes our perceptions. He points out how we think we act using our free will but we are often stuck on a set of brain circuits that control our thinking and behavior until we realize and overcome it. He explains further how the self we know is largely an artificial one. It is not real. We only believe it is, and our delusion tricks us into perpetually limiting ourselves.

As an illustration, think of those people in past centuries who believed the world was flat. It is understandable why they thought so. They looked toward the horizon and it looked flat. They believed what they saw, and so few were keen on long sailing expeditions because they thought they might fall off the edge of the world! They could not get past the *illusion,* they limited themselves.

Likewise, you limit yourself if you allow the appearance of the outer world to dictate who you are. You can overcome this trap by identifying with your Higher Self.

However, you do not have to directly perceive your Higher Self to identify with it. Nor do you have to see visions to receive the extraordinary benefits of working with your Higher Self. You can take small steps right at this moment and work your way ever higher until you reach that ultimate level of awareness. It is on these steps that the strategies in this book are focused.

What Alignment Means, and How It Helps You to Manifest Masterfully

BEFORE WE DISCUSS THE STRATEGIES for aligning with the Higher Self, it is first a good idea to know what is meant by alignment.

Have you ever driven a car with a steering column out of alignment? When you hold the steering wheel to go straight ahead, the misaligned vehicle veers off course. And to keep from crashing you are forced to adjust. If the car's steering column had been aligned properly, the car would have gone exactly where you steered it with little effort.

When we are out of alignment with the intentions of the Higher Self, we start out with a desire we wish to manifest but things often go wrong. Before we know it, we have veered off course and have manifested things we never intended. However, when we take certain steps to align with the Higher Self we can manifest what we desire with remarkable precision and speed.

Here is what I have realized alignment with the Higher Self means:

* Alignment means increasing your awareness and understanding of your Higher Self through whatever means are available. At first, attempts at alignment are based on principles that come from other people (or books) who share their insights about the Higher Self. However, all their insights should be taken cautiously (including the ones in this book), because people can misinterpret principles based on their limited level of development and their unique relationship to their Higher Self. What is good for them at that time may not be good for you.

Instead, it is better to establish your own sense of alignment and rapport with your Higher Self, and then do things based on the principles *you* recognize and understand. These principles may be in harmony with your religion or in opposition to it. It is up to *you* to decide what is right for you, even when it's at variance with your religion.

* Alignment means developing a new self-image based on the Higher Self rather than on the false ego. Your Higher Self is the Real You, unadulterated by society, circumstances, or the false ego. Therefore, alignment implies that you establish a new vision about who you are. It means you must discard, layer by layer, the false masks that have defined you in the past, and see

yourself in a whole new way. When you do that, the image of your Real Self will begin to emerge.

Alignment means letting go of desires that conflict with your Higher Self. Desire is a mighty and wondrous thing when it is properly interpreted and directed. But many of your desires may be misinterpretations or distortions of what your Higher Self wants for you. You must learn to let go of desires which are contrary to your highest good. So to realign those with your Higher Self, you need to let go of and perhaps learn how to reinterpret those desires. That way, you will start to reflect a greater wisdom and understanding.

Alignment means learning to know the Voice of your Higher Self. The Voice of your Higher Self guides you on your path so that you may fulfill your destiny in this life. By *voice*, I do not mean an actual audible one. To quote the character Hermione Granger from *Harry Potter and the Chamber of Secrets*: "Hearing voices, even in the wizarding world, isn't a good sign."

However, I will admit there were times when I heard an audible voice. Once, while meditating, I had trouble identifying a color which appeared in my energy field or *aura*. And I heard a voice firmly, calmly, and distinctly say: "It is gold." I was so startled that I immediately snapped out of the meditation and marveled at what happened. I wondered if it was the actual voice of my Higher

Self or if it was the voice of someone observing me on another plane. To this day, I am not sure who it was.

You are not *looking* for audible voices though. There are mental impressions that will come to you from your Higher Self. But remember that even now this Voice is always with you, though it can be tricky to discriminate between it and the many voices coming from the false ego, from psychic chatter or other sources.

To recall the importance of tuning into the Higher Self, I listen to "The Voice," by The Moody Blues. The lyrics to that song say more than I could about the meaning of hearing the Voice of the Higher Self.

* Alignment means life and growth. When we align with the Higher Self, we are aligning with the flow of life and achieving deep, personal growth. Alignment brings peace to your manifestations and to your future. It does not imply that all your manifestations will be perfect though, because you and I are incomplete and our manifestations will reflect that. And it does not mean unfortunate things will never happen either, because we all have life lessons and karma to deal with. When we perform an unbalanced action, it eventually returns and manifests as an unfortunate event. Even when our personal actions are aligned with the Higher Self, there are

other types of karma that can and do affect us: group karma, family karma, racial karma, national karma, and the karma of all humanity. However, through your own balanced alignment with your Higher Self, you can offset some of the negative karma and even help to transform your group karma.

Four Simple Steps Toward Alignment

Now that you know what is meant by alignment, let us consider steps you can take to establish it. They are simple, and you can start them right away.

* *Step 1: Recognize the need for alignment, and desire it.* Since you are reading this book, it is likely you already know something may be misaligned and you want to do something about it. It may be that you sense your life could be improved. You might be missing something. Perhaps you have attempted to manifest desires with poor results or results that backfired. If that is the case, be glad! Those perceived failures are necessary feedback you need to search for something else, something more. And this will lead you right to your Higher Self. The more you learn about the benefits of alignment, the more you will desire it, focus on it, and manifest ways to establish it.

* *Step 2: Start where you are.* Perfect alignment may be a long way off for you. You and I do not have to be perfectly aligned to inch closer to the ultimate alignment. We can begin right where we are, whether our lives are prosperous or in shambles or somewhere in between. The Emerald Tablet of Hermes tells us much about attaining perfect alignment. The Emerald Tablet is an ancient hermetic document that speaks in the language of spiritual alchemy. It is where the saying, "as above, so below" comes from. If you examine it closely, I promise it will pay off.

* *Step 3: Pay attention.* Although it appears that the desire to align comes from you, its true source is your Higher Self. That is, it is your Higher Self who first seeks you! That desire of yours is really a response to it. Therefore, pay close attention to the strange coincidences in your life—which are called *synchronicities*—that lead you to discover how your Higher Self wants you to align. The answers could appear through songs, chance meetings, conversations, published writings, texts or through your own contemplation or intuition.

* *Step 4: Seek ways to align.* If you give it some thought, you will discover many ways to draw closer to your Higher Self. As your desire for alignment grows, so too will your intention grow to find ways to make that happen. You will

manifest strategies that make sense to you. For example, since you manifested this book your ability to draw the information you need is already here.

Higher Self Alignment Strategies

THE REMAINDER OF THIS BOOK discusses strategies that work for me and for those I have coached. Some of them are easy to do; others are more challenging. As you read about each one, there may be times when you experience rushes of excitement or quickenings of the soul. If that happens, pay close attention. It may indicate your Higher Self wants you to immediately incorporate that strategy.

But even if that kind of quickening does not happen, each of the following strategies is tested and proven and will take you in the right direction. You may decide to implement all the strategies or choose the ones that are most appealing. Use your intuition. Trust yourself. You will get what you need.

On to the strategies.

Alignment Strategy 1: Think About Your Higher Self Each Day

By far the easiest way to reach toward alignment is to contemplate your Higher Self daily. For example, in the short time you have been reading this book your mind has started to process the concepts and information about the Higher Self.

> *Simply thinking about your Higher Self*
> *and your relationship with it is enough*
> *to propel you toward alignment.*

It is even okay if you are not sure yet whether you believe in a Higher Self. At this time, you might only be ready to consider that it might work for you in the future. You might even finish this book and forget about your Higher Self for a while, only to come back to it month or years from now. You might be ready then to have a revelation that allows you to see and understand the reality of your Higher Self.

If you believe or know that your Higher Self is real, then you have reached a point where you are ready to realize and understand more. And the more you think about your Higher Self, the stronger and faster your awareness and understanding will grow.

Books like this show you the door, but you are the one who needs to walk through it.

There are other books you can read to learn more about this subject. Here are just a few to get you started:

* *The Power of Now* by Eckhart Tolley

* *The Secret Science Behind Miracles* by Max Freedom Long

* *21st Century Mage: Bring the Divine Down to Earth* by Jason Augustus Newcomb

* *The One Year Manual: Twelve Steps to Spiritual Enlightenment* by Israel Regardie

* *From Your Higher Being* by Tharyn Taylor

* *The Higher Powers of Mind and Spirit* by Ralph Waldo Trine

* *The Impersonal Life* by Joseph Benner

You may have noticed that I did not include the Bible, the Koran, the Torah, or any other "holy" texts in this list. About this subject, holy books can be confusing and counterproductive. For instance, the Bible is a powerful collection of ancient knowledge, but deciphering it is a herculean task. Most of its deeper wisdom is veiled from the casual reader, which makes it difficult to be of practical value for our purposes. Therefore, in your initial stages of pursuing alignment with your Higher Self, I caution you about using traditional holy books. Ancient scriptures may be useful later, but for the beginner I do not recommend them.

Alignment Strategy 2: Redirect Your Subconscious to Your Higher Self

Your Higher Self has always been with you, but you may not have known it. So far you might have depended on the communication between your conscious and subconscious mind to manifest things. And because your reality might have been based on the appearance of things, it was easy for your manifestations to go wrong.

Many of the things we desire to manifest are based on surface values and a limited perspective. Your Higher Self, on the other hand, has a broad perspective on all aspects of your life. Its understanding of the world is accurate.

So, this strategy is about shifting your inner awareness to align communication between the three aspects of your mind: your conscious mind, your subconscious mind, and your Higher Self.

The key is to redirect your subconscious mind to pay attention to your Higher Self, because all that you learn and hear from your Higher Self comes to you through your subconscious mind.

Your conscious mind deals with your everyday awareness. It has the power to make choices and to influence your subconscious mind.

The subconscious is the level of the mind that is below the threshold of your daily awareness, and it carries out the directives coming from the conscious mind to manifest your desires.

There is a third aspect to your being, and that is your Higher Self. In *The Manifestation Matrix,* I introduced a Tarot card as a tool for successful manifestation. Meditating on some of those cards is an outstanding way to help you achieve alignment with your Higher Self. The Tarot has gotten a bad reputation because it has been used as a plaything for fortune-telling. Religions are often afraid of it too, having been told it is a tool of the devil. That is far from the truth.

There is a deeper purpose to the power of the Tarot few people understand. The Tarot may be used to stimulate and organize the powers of your mind and body. It can be used to help you understand and connect with your Higher Self. Through imagery and symbolism, the Tarot can convey ideas to your inner mind that go way beyond words. I honestly do not know of a more versatile tool for psychological or metaphysical change and development.

The Lovers card in the Tarot from the Rider-Waite deck reveals an accurate and working relationship between you and your Higher Self. It depicts an Adam and Eve-like scene with an Angel hovering overhead. The man represents the conscious mind and the woman represents the subconscious. The Angel, who is the archangel Raphael, symbolizes the Higher Self. The Lovers card reveals that *it is through your subconscious that you initially perceive and communicate with your Higher Self.*

In the card, you see that the conscious self does not directly gaze at the Higher Self. It gets information as it looks to the subconscious which can perceive the Higher Self and act as a guide. However, here is what you must keep in mind:

> *To manifest good things, you must consciously direct and train your subconscious mind to pay attention to your Higher Self.*

Otherwise, your subconscious will pay attention to the chaotic whims of your personality and sometimes manifest unfortunate things.

By merely looking at the card five minutes a day, your inner mind will get the hint to redirect its attention to the Higher Self so you may align with it through the power of visual suggestion. It may take several weeks of consistency with this technique to create this result, but it is worth investing that time.

Other Tarot cards may also be used to better align with your Higher Self. One symbol signifying this is an Angel as in the Temperance card of the Case Deck, where you will see the Archangel Michael controlling a lion and an eagle. The card reveals that the Higher Self transforms you, and is at work during every phase of your life. I use this card frequently to remind myself I am not alone during any activity at any time. It calms me down during times of struggle and hardship. And it assures me that everything serves a purpose, even if I cannot immediately see it.

Another card of particular note is the Judgment Tarot card from the Case Deck. While direct perception of the Higher Self may be a long way off for you, this card depicts what happens when it finally occurs. Looking at this card regularly makes a potent suggestion to your inner mind about your goal: to experience conscious awareness that your Higher Self is the Real You. Once that is achieved, alignment is complete and perpetual. And that will make manifesting the absolute best infinitely easier and more pleasurable. Perhaps you can see why I like to meditate with this card.

Please note that there are many Tarot decks available. While some are very creative and beautiful, be careful which one you use as a meditation tool. Images are powerful, and if the symbolism presented by the Tarot artist is confusing or misaligned you may send the wrong message to your inner mind and do more harm than good.

I can only recommend two tarot decks at this time: the Rider-Waite Deck or the Case Deck (which I prefer).

Alignment Strategy 3: Practice the Presence of Your Higher Self

Your Higher Self knows everything you do, everything you think, everything you want. It has been bringing you to a point where you are ready to consciously develop your relationship with it to experience empowered living. One way to do that is to mentally and emotionally reach out to your Higher Self.

I have learned to do that by bringing my awareness of my Higher Self with me always, even when what I desire to manifest is questionable. There was a time when I knew I was engaging in activities which might not be in alignment with my Higher Self, and because I was ashamed I chose to hide from my it.

At some point, I recognized the obvious. There is no hiding from my Higher Self. It's there whether I want it to be or not. It knows exactly what I am up to. It knows my motives and the reasons behind them better than I do. It also knows that some part of me must *need* the experience I seek to manifest, even if that experience might not be ideal. So instead of ignoring my Higher Self, I consciously invited my Higher Self to be with me during all activities, whatever they were.

The results have been surprising. For example, for a while I had a habit of looking at internet pornography. Are you shocked? Well, it is true and

I promised myself I would tell you the truth even when it might be embarrassing. Anyway, though I knew that watching porn was not the best activity for me to align with my Higher Self, I pretended my Higher Self was not around so I could watch it.

However, something unexpected happened one day when I said to my Higher Self, "Be with me as I watch porn." The first thing I noticed was I enjoyed that activity without shame. And maybe for the first time in my life, I could fully enjoy it.

Here is the thing: *within days of inviting my Higher Self into the activity, my interest in pornography began to fade!* Quitting that activity was not my intention at all. However, it was my Higher Self who moved me *beyond* that immature activity.

Whatever you decide to do or to manifest, invite your Higher Self into that activity the way you might invite a very good friend. Then, embrace the activity knowing your Higher Self is right there with you, and seeing it through your eyes. Pay attention to any shifts in your thinking during and after the activity. All of this will help you to align with your Higher Self better over time.

I do not claim that everyone can overcome addictions so easily, but it will make you more receptive to your Higher Self. And when you can respond, you will be able to move beyond that addictive behavior. Maybe you will find something else you were searching for all along, and could not recognize until you gave up that addiction.

Alignment Strategy 4: Manifest in Harmony with Cosmic Cycles

> "Everything flows out and in;
> everything has its tides..."
>
> —*the Kybalion*

We are creative beings, and our thoughts and actions are responsible for what we manifest in our lives. This is true for those who understand the principles of manifestation, and even for those who are unaware of it.

However, those of us who are aware can observe there are certain times when manifesting in specific areas of life is easier because the Universe operates by what may be called Cosmic Law. And part of this Law reveals that everything runs in a pattern, a rhythm, or a *cycle*.

The Higher Self is certainly attuned to cosmic cycles. When you manifest in alignment with them, you are automatically in tune with your Higher Self. You will then find your manifestation efforts will work more cohesively.

For instance, there are favorable times for pursuing success with a new personal or professional project. When you are in harmony with the rhythm of the Universe, the project flows smoothly and things just fall into place. But if you are not in harmony, you encounter countless obstacles, are frustrated, and might even fail.

Here is an example of being not in harmony or balanced with cosmic timing. I planned to write and release this book months earlier, but the ideas and words just would not come to me. So, I waited for the hands on the cosmic clock to turn, and finally they did. My thoughts organized easily enough, and expressed themselves as the words you are reading. No more struggling.

I used what most people refer to as *intuition* to figure out when the time was right to manifest this book. So, if you are also highly intuitive, you can use your own intuition to determine whether you are in harmony with the cosmic cycles.

But there are other ways to estimate cosmic timing if your intuition is unreliable. The best way I know is through astrology, which charts the relationship between the positions of the stars and planets and how it affects human behaviors.

I used to think astrology was nonsense until my mother, who is a farmer's daughter, told me a story. There was a time when she did not believe in astrology either, even though her mother and father did. To get the best harvest, they would plant crops according to certain astrological signs from the *Farmer's Almanac.*

One day in my mother's own garden, and against my grandmother's advice, my mother planted green beans in the *sign of the flower.* Here is the surprising thing: when the crop manifested, they flowered so much that there were hardly any beans at all.

After that experience, my mother never doubted astrology.

I resisted astrology because I believed that when those kinds of forecasts are made, it creates a suggestion in our minds which can influence our emotions and the actions we take.

Also, I thought horoscopes were too general to be of any value. That opinion was about to change.

A friend of mine, a well-respected research scientist, sent me a link to a website which offers a free birthday horoscope report with cycles and trends for the coming year. It impressed me so much I purchased the full report.

When I downloaded that report, I was stunned. It was not a listing of vague statements. It predicted correctly how issues with my mother would dominate my year. It warned me of my own specific health issues, the ones that existed and would come. That amazed me too.

Those are just two of many examples which have caused me to reassess astrology's value as a tool. It allows me to know what cycles I am approaching so that I can manifest things in harmony with them. If you are interested in such a report, the website is: https://cafeastrology.com.

Now, if astrology is not your thing, there are other ways to assess your cosmic cycles for manifestation. For example, there is a classic metaphysical book called *Self-Mastery and Fate with the Cycles of Life* by H. Spencer Lewis, which goes into detail to help you chart your own personal and professional cycles. Lewis was the leader of the Rosicrucian Order (AMORC) in the early 20th century. His work can benefit modern readers too because he had a knowledge of life, mysticism and reality which is profound and relevant even today.

Alignment Strategy 5: Recalibrate Your Desires

I can imagine there are many things you want to manifest: more money, a workplace promotion, more travel opportunities, your health improved, or a better social life. Those could be just for starters. And you want to start yesterday, right?

However, before you pursue any manifestation goal, determine whether it's in alignment with the will of your Higher Self who is the true source of all your desires—from the most inconsequential to the grandest.

Always remember that nothing originates from the level of your personality. It begins at the higher levels of consciousness. We sometimes misinterpret what the Higher Self intends.

We do this because we are immature, evolving beings. To illustrate, have you ever been at your grocery store and observed young children as they reach and beg for sugary treats? The colorful packaging, the sweet smells, the smiles. They want everything that appeals to their senses and they want it *now*. Whenever the parents say "No," often the children endlessly cry and carry on. Of course, there is nothing wrong with a sweet treat now and again. However, the children would become unhealthy and fat and spoiled if the parents often said yes to all that junk. The children are not in a place to understand all of this because they are still immature.

In the 1984 movie, *Labyrinth*, there is a poignant scene where the character Sarah finds herself in a junkyard. She has amnesia, but is driven to look for something though she cannot recall exactly what. Sarah meets a junk lady who piles toys and trinkets upon her and tricks her into thinking they are what she has been searching for all along. When the spell breaks, Sarah realizes it is *all* junk! None of it matters.

She remembers she has gone through "dangers untold and hardships unnumbered" to save her baby brother <u>Toby</u> from turning into a goblin. Then, Sarah makes her way through the Labyrinth to learn what is truly important and to reclaim her power and grow up.

When it comes to manifestation, there is a strong tendency to think we want to fill our lives with adult toys and trinkets such as fancy cars, lavish houses, and designer clothes. Often such desires are misplaced though. Could it be that, like Sarah, each of us is looking for something in our turbulent lives and just cannot remember what it is? Have we fooled ourselves into believing that a life of material luxury is what we need to manifest?

The truth is you do not need to align with your Higher Self to manifest those things. If you concentrate long and hard enough, and then act in the material world it is entirely possible you could manifest enough to go "...play with your toys and your costumes...," to quote the character Jareth (who was played by the late David Bowie) from the same *Labyrinth* movie. If that is what you want and all you want, then go for it. I do not say that to shame you. I have done it and sometimes it went well, at other times badly.

Here is another example. In my 20s, I wanted to have a much better body to look good on the beach and get more attention and respect. Yes, it was pure male vanity. Just working out in the gym was not getting me what I wanted, so I sought out performance-enhancing substances to help me manifest it. I knew this was probably not in alignment with my Higher Self, but I did it anyway. Bad idea. Within a week or two of taking those substances, I became ill and felt terrible for weeks.

That was not the worst example. In the early 2000s, I became impatient with my metaphysical growth. So, I decided to perform several metaphysical techniques I found in books to help me raise my Kundalini. I ignored the nagging feeling that this was foolish. Though I experienced some remarkable abilities during that time, my body was not ready to handle the "life force energy." Over the course of a few weeks, I experienced so many disturbing things. Nerve tremors. Light-headedness. An aching at the base of my spine that would not go away. Like I was in a strange perpetual trance and feeling ungrounded. Fortunately, my Higher Self intervened.

One evening, after performing those techniques, I felt a strong presence in the room with me. Suddenly, out of my own mouth, came the stern warning, "If you do not stop you will die." I was taken aback, but took that message seriously and discontinued the techniques I had been using. Since then, I have become more patient and cautious about the development of my supersensory powers.

Perhaps you may have read about techniques that promise to quickly awaken the Kundalini to give you some sort of powers. Be very careful with them.

The dormant forces in your body are
real and extremely potent, and without
proper supervision you may injure
yourself beyond repair. I do not
want that to happen to you.
Learn from my mistake.

With a little soul-searching, you may discover it is the experience and feeling that you really desire. It is not the "magical powers" you want, but the discovery of your unique abilities. It is not more money you need, but the feeling of luxury and security you want. It is not fame you crave, but the need to feel valued by others.

To align any desire with your Higher Self, ask yourself these valuable questions:

1. "Is this really a good thing I want, or is it just another shiny object of little true value?"

2. "Is it something that will help me to grow stronger mentally, physically, and spiritually or will it satisfy only my vanity?"

3. "Is the manifestation of this desire good for everyone or good just for me?"

Whenever you find a problem, remember how that the root desire is never bad: it is only your poor interpretation of it that's in question. Reconsider your original desire, and then recalibrate it so you can align with what you know about your Higher

Self. That way, you prevent yourself from wasting time collecting "junk" and you will aim positively toward what will make you truly happy.

Alignment Strategy 6: Ask Your Higher Self for Verification

One of my favorite ways to make sure my desires are in alignment with my Higher Self is to ask for verification.

> *With eyes open or closed, I ask my Higher Self silently or aloud, "Is this what we want to manifest?" Then I go on my way as I wait for verification to show up.*

Alignment confirmation rarely comes in the form of a vision, a supernatural event, a booming voice from the sky or anything startling. More likely it comes in the form of one or more synchronicities (remarkable coincidences) pointing to the verification of the desire.

Your Higher Mind arranges these coincidences as a way of saying, "Yes, I AM here and I approve." For instance, you might start to notice car license plates with messages that stand out to you which affirm your desires. You might notice how someone randomly starts a conversation with you about the Higher Self or something related to your desires. Or, it could even come in the form of an unexpected solution to one of your significant challenges. Whatever they are, those verifications will seem important enough to stand out to you.

Remember when I told you about the song by the Moody Blues, called *The Voice*? During the writing of this book, I decided to listen to that song again, and when I did, I experienced what I call "inner leaps of joy." I felt electric charges of pleasure and enthusiasm surging through my body and mind. That was a strong verification and support coming from my Higher Self to confirm the manifestation of this book.

This wasn't the first time I felt this. I know that it was my Higher Self making itself known to me.

Interestingly, you may also get clear indications when your Higher Self considers a desire unwise. Not long ago, a woman wrote to me asking what I thought of her desire to manifest great lottery winnings. Since she already had an awareness of her Higher Self, I asked her to meditate about it. Days later, she again wrote and said that when she asked her Higher Self about this she got an unpleasant and sick feeling. She felt that it meant seeking money through the lottery was unwise to do now. This is an example of the Higher Self communicating when a desire is *out of alignment*.

Remember that your Higher Self knows everything you think, even before it reaches your conscious mind. So, it is aware of your level of awareness at this time of your life. It's happy to provide exactly what you need to keep your feet on the path of growth and life.

Because your Higher Self already knows if you need encouragement through verification, you can start to look for it from now on without having to formally ask for it. However, you may address your Higher Self as you would a respected elder and it will suffice. To do that, I would suggest you use words like these:

*"Higher Self, Higher Mind, Higher
Soul, grant me verification that the
desire in my mind is in alignment with
your will and the highest good of all.
Thank you."*

Once you have asked this, your job is to patiently yet expectantly wait and look for a reply. You might receive your answer right there during the meditation, later or when you least expect it. When you have received your answer, it is up to you what to do next. Here is a question for you: Do you listen or ignore the influence and advice of your Higher Self?

The Higher Self never *insists* that you obey it. Instead, it is like a permissive parent. Often, like children we want what we want. And, recognizing this, the Higher Self often allows you to do what you want even if it leads to unpleasantness because that is part of your growth to maturity.

Alignment Strategy 7: Tower of Light Meditation

Early in my years as a hypnotherapist and metaphysical coach in the 1990s, I created a meditation called "The Tower of Light Meditation." I believe it is one of the most powerful meditations I have ever created. It can effectively help you to align with your Higher Self. I am pleased to offer it here.

The meditation first relaxes you as you perform it. The imagery gives your inner mind the suggestion that you are in the very presence of your Higher Self, a being of light and love.

I was inspired to create it after a remarkable experience I had while meditating on my Higher Self. I was really reaching out to it for a direct and strong awareness of its Presence. I remember pleading before the meditation: "Throw me a bone, will ya?"

The meditation started, and to my astonishment I started to feel something strange behind my meditation chair. I stopped what I was doing, and got up to look behind the chair. There seemed to be nothing there, so I looked around it and up at the ceiling. Then I saw it. Up in the corner of the ceiling of the meditation room I saw what I can only describe as a shining white star which blazed brightly and sent out radiant beams of light and warmth. But even more remarkable was the all-enveloping feeling of Love I could sense coming from the light. While it should have filled me with fear, instead I felt safety and love.

I knew this was no ordinary star or abstract energy. I knew it was a Higher Being who had come to answer my plea. And yet no words came from it. It was simply *there*, and wanted me to know it.

I have never forgotten that experience, nor have I experienced anything like it since. However, it was more than enough to affirm to me that Higher Beings do exist and that I should continue to pursue alignment with my Higher Self.

I do not promise you will experience anything like that by employing the following meditation. And I am not even saying you should seek out experiences like mine because they can lead to chasing fantastic phenomena rather than concentrating on manifesting a better life. You may or may not feel anything specific during the meditation. However, the power of the suggestions contained in the narrative will work on your subconscious long after the meditation is finished.

I created an audio meditation from the narrative called "The Presence of Love," however I prefer the following written, self-guided meditation.

A long time ago I discovered that it's easy to put yourself into a relaxed, meditative state merely by reading words designed for that purpose. To be effective, the key is to read them aloud and rather slowly and really take the time to absorb the meaning of the words.

While you may record the meditation, and play it back with your eyes closed, there is no need to do so. If you speak aloud in a relaxed tone (not a whisper), your voice combined with the words of the narrative will place you in a conducive meditative state. I prefer the read aloud method because it keeps your attention where it should be always and is, therefore, likely to be more effective.

I recommend you perform this meditation in a safe and quiet place where you will not be disturbed. You may need to perform the meditation once or twice a week for several weeks to notice any change in the awareness of your Higher Self. But stick with it, and it will help you succeed.

Read the following meditation aloud, and it will bring you many benefits. The words in parenthesis contain instructions for you to follow (you do not need to read those words aloud though).

The Tower of Light
Meditation

(best when read aloud)

"As I read these words slowly and carefully, I gently direct my body and my thinking to now calm down as I draw a gentle, deep breath.

(Draw a breath and release it slowly.)

"Calm down now.

"With every passing moment and every word I read, I relax deeper and deeper . . . until I feel completely at ease.

"I pretend everything around me helps me to relax. If there are sounds around me, above me or below me, they only remind me of how good I feel. I imagine I sit in the most comfortable and supportive chair.

"In a moment, I will draw and release another gentle breath. As I release it, I will decide to relax twice as deeply.

(Draw a breath and release it slowly.)

"I can feel myself entering a deep and powerful meditative state of mind and body. It is a wonderful feeling, so I let go and allow myself to go there.

"And as I do, it becomes so easy for me to imagine pictures in my mind.

"I imagine I am walking along a cobble-stoned path winding through a beautiful lush forest. Tall trees surround me with signs of friendly wildlife everywhere.

"I picture crossing a sturdy stone bridge that passes over a gentle stream of clear, sparkling water.

"On the other side of the bridge, I step out into a large open meadow full of tall and large sunflowers that reach up happily toward the sky.

"I see ahead at the top of a hill a majestic tower. The tower, as it reflects the sun, seems to glow with a pristine splendor. Vibrant green grass gently circles the tower as wild peacocks graze along.

"I notice a pair of large and heavy oak doors at the base of the tower which open on their own as I approach them. I am in a trance as I pass through the doors.

"I see a spiral staircase leading up, and I imagine climbing its stone stairs. Up and around . . . up and around. As I climb, I notice the painted inner walls of the tower turning from deep blue violet to royal blue. And, as I climb higher, and more up and around, I notice the walls becoming lighter and brighter, as I start to feel lighter and brighter.

"As I near the top of the stairway, I see a magnificent door embossed with an unusual symbol etched in pure and solid white-gold. It is the symbol for my highest conception of my Higher Self. Thinking about this symbol in this way grants me access to all the thoughts and feelings it represents which are associated with my Higher Self.

(Take a moment to picture that embossed symbol on the door.)

"My concentration on the symbol causes it to glow. Then the door magically opens, and the light spills increasingly onto the stairway.

"Finally, I walk through the door and onto the stone tower rooftop. I am greeted by dazzling golden sunlight so bright it takes a while for my eyes to adjust. As they do, I begin to sense a loving Presence on the tower rooftop with me.

"I see nothing but I can feel the Presence all around, and it is very powerful. I can feel waves of compassion, loving-kindness and unconditional true love penetrating my whole being.

"This Presence is strong and protective, and gentle and nurturing. It is the Presence of my Higher Self. It is real, and it knows me personally and intimately.

"I look for the source of the Presence, but I can see no one. However, I do notice how the sun shines directly overhead so brightly now that I must avert my eyes. Instead, I look at how much it illuminates everything around me.

"And as I continue to search for the source of this Presence, I feel certain there is some Being here with me. It is so close, so very close, it's as if I am bathed in the very Presence of Love.

"It carries with it the feeling that I am treasured, appreciated and deeply cared for. Somehow, I know this Presence wants the highest experience of Joy for me.

"It is a Presence that washes away sorrow, anger, fear. And instead I feel joy, lightheartedness, and optimism.

"I seem to know how much this Presence finds me deeply beautiful and special in every way, in every sense. Somehow, I know it is all based on absolute truth.

"And as I look down at my hands and arms, I see my upper limbs are radiant with light—and depth. It magnifies my experience so much I feel I can see the very atoms of my body. And, at the very center of each atom, are tiny points of the brightest white light that both absorb and reflect light all around. I know that it is from within these tiny points that this Presence flows.

"Yes, the source of this living Presence of my Higher Self lives outside and inside of me at the same time. This means it is always with me. There is never a time when I am truly alone. The times I thought I was most alone, the Presence of my Higher Self was there, even when I could not see it or feel it. And it will always be there, because it is the very Source of my being. I am never separate from it at any time. We are One.

"The loving Presence does not demand or expect anything from me, but its very Presence transforms me into a better person in every way. I have only to realize that Love is here, right now.

"And as I increasingly acknowledge its strong presence in my life through simple awareness, I draw on its power to heal me, to help me, and to express Joy and manifest prosperity in ever greater measure. The more I recognize the living Presence of Love daily, the more it finds clear expression in me and through me.

"As I look out over the tower at the surrounding lands below, I see the tops of trees, the green meadows and the valleys. I see the roads that lead to towns and cities, and rivers and mountains in the distance. The sun shines warmly on all the lands below which represent the landscape of my everyday life and world.

"I am ready to return to the land below, refreshed and invigorated. I can return to the top of the tower anytime I wish to remind myself of the Presence of my Higher Self. But even as I go back through the door which closes behind me, and I begin to descend the spiral staircase, I feel the Presence of my Higher Self coming with me.

"I walk down the staircase. I feel myself going down and around . . . down and around. The stone stairs and the walls go from a bright royal blue to a deep blue violet until I reach the bottom where the floor is an earthy stone brown. But that doesn't dampen my spirit, because the Presence of my Higher Self is within me even in the ordinary world.

"I finally reach the bottom step, and I leave the majestic tower of light knowing I may return whenever I wish. I walk down the hill that brought me here, and I can feel the solid ground beneath my feet. And now, I am ready to return to my everyday life and the many tasks I want and need to accomplish. My Higher Self is here to help me do them successfully.

"As I count to five, I gently direct my mind to return completely to the everyday way of thinking and feeling.

"One . . . two . . . three . . . four . . . five.

"This meditation is finished and I am ready to continue."

(End of meditation.)

Alignment Strategy 8: Work on Yourself

As you move forward with your pursuit of alignment, it may become clear that you are not trying to get anything you do not already have. All the power you will ever have is here now, including that of your Higher Self. You do not need to add anything to manifest abundance and prosperity.

On the contrary, you need to remove what obscures the power you already possess and anything that impedes the relationship with your Higher Self which already exists.

> *The obstacles in your life are mental ones. They are incorrect patterns of thought and behavior which impede you from manifesting with full power and potential. By working on improving yourself psychologically, you clear away whatever obstructs you energetically from aligning with your Higher Self.*

You may think that thoughts are just thoughts and emotions are just feelings. However, your thoughts and emotions, particularly those which show up as habit patterns, influence how well you can align with your Higher Self—and on what you manifest.

It is time to learn how to let go of the fear, anger, prejudice, bigotry, envy, self-pity, and judgment of your fellow human beings. When I was a Christian fundamentalist, I felt completely justified in my prejudice, disapproval, and condemnation of all who did not believe as I did. Little did I understand that my spiritual pride had formed a hard, energetic shell through which little light from my Higher Self could penetrate. This was very hard for me to break out of because I did not even recognize my own hypocrisy at that time.

Fortunately, my Higher Self arranged for me to fall in love with someone with a different faith and of whom my religion disapproved. It forced me to question my belief system. In time, I came out of that self-imposed trap.

Do not get me wrong. Traditional religion can be a wonderful thing and may be part of your journey as it was for me, but it can also block you from the very thing you are trying to achieve. It is worth examining carefully.

Facing our own shortcomings can be uncomfortable and difficult. It is uncomfortable because we want to believe that we are good people, so we rationalize the thoughts and actions that suggest we are otherwise. It is difficult because the work required to truly transform undesirable thoughts and behaviors can be daunting. But as a wise metaphysical friend used to say, "It is the only game in town."

If you plan to align with your Higher Self and to become capable of manifesting your absolute best, then you must face yourself boldly and get to work to change what's necessary. It may be a long journey, but it will be worthwhile.

When you want to take stock of your life and become healthier spiritually, it does not help you to blame your mom or dad, or your ex, or your ethnicity or gender or sexuality or anything else for where you are. It is up to you, with the help of your Higher Self, to transform your mind to manifest wonderful things without those former self-imposed obstructions.

My guess is that working to better yourself is not new to you. Here you are reading a self-help book. So, if you want to work on yourself, keep reading these kinds of books that appeal to you.

I recently read an article putting down self-help books, claiming they help very few people and they are just meant to fatten the wallets of their authors. What a cynical perspective! It takes a great deal of effort and time to write even a short book like this one. I do not write my books to get rich, and I think that's true for most authors. What we want to do is share our experiences and ideas because we believe we can be helpful to our readers. It is so gratifying when we receive emails from people who tell us how we have helped to change their lives because of our books.

Another way to work on yourself is through a good psychologist or therapist. Their goal is not to judge you or tell you how to live. Their objective is to help you discover what you want and to remove the psychological and emotional obstacles that might keep you from it. Even short-term therapy can be greatly illuminating.

Another way to help you clear manifestation obstructions is to make up with people you have harmed, mentally or physically. Your subconscious remembers everything you have ever done. And while your Higher Self does not withhold any good thing from you, your subconscious may feel you do not deserve prosperity because you have harmed others. Therefore, it is wise to clear your conscience of all wrongdoing and guilt. Also, you should sincerely let others know how you regret any distress you may have caused.

If this cannot be done, then you could perform some charity or good deed that might in some way relate to it. For instance, if you bullied someone but were unable to reach that person to express genuine regret, you might contribute to a battered wives group or you might volunteer your time, for instance. This will probably be good enough for your subconscious mind to absolve you of the wrongdoing, and to permit the correct alignment with your Higher Self. Let's call it a sort of balancing of the scales.

Alignment Strategy 9: Higher Self Manifestation Technique

When I studied Huna, I learned a great technique for manifesting with my Higher Self. Since then, I have modified it to better match my own understanding of manifestation. Let me share the Higher Self Manifestation Technique with you.

In my second book in this series, *The Manifestation Matrix*, I revealed a nine-step technique for manifesting a goal. While I stand by that formula for general manifesting, the Higher Self was not the focus of that book.

When the following technique is put into practice, it encourages good alignment with the Higher Self as you concentrate on your manifestation goal in a specific way.

However, it is first vital that you accept you have a Higher Self or else the technique is likely to fail. There is no fooling your subconscious about this. Either you believe it or you don't. If you do not, then I recommend you work first with some of the other techniques in this book to gain your awareness of your Higher Self. Then, you will be prepared to work with the following technique and be successful.

1. Carefully consider what you want and make a statement of desire. Choose *one* desire you wish to manifest. Be certain it is something you realistically believe can happen, and that it will harm no one and will help all the people concerned. Then, create a statement that describes what you want. For example, "I want to manifest opportunities for a job in Human Resources that pays at least $60,000 annually with excellent health benefits." If you know exactly what job you want, then describe it in your statement clearly. The more specific you can be, the better.

2. *Collect a surplus of Vital Energy.* The type of force that can propel your thoughts into manifestation is sometimes called Vital Energy, Mana, Lee, Prana, Chi, or by some other name. It is the essential Life Force itself and it's found everywhere. There are many ways to ensure that you have an ample supply available for manifesting. For many examples on how to acquire it, please see my other books in this series: *The Manifestation Manifesto* or *The Manifestation Matrix.* A quick and easy method to accumulate a generous supply of vital energy is to smoothly draw a deep breath, and without straining, hold it for a while, and then slowly release it. Repeat this procedure six to ten times.

3. *Daydream or visualize your intended outcome.* Relax with your eyes closed or open and ponder what life will be like when your goal has come true. Do not concern yourself with how it will

manifest because your Higher Self will decide that for you. Take several minutes with this step. If you are doing it right, you will feel as if your goal is already a reality.

4. Focus on your Higher Self. While remaining relaxed, whether sitting or standing, bring your Higher Self to mind. Meditate on it, contemplate it, revere it, and mentally reach out to it. If possible, rouse the emotion of love for your Higher Self. If you have not reached the point where you have come to love your Higher Self, then just use your desire for connection with it. You might feel a swell of emotion when you do this sincerely and often enough. But even if you don't feel anything, just trust, or imagine that your Higher Self is present. That will be enough to take you a long way.

5. Transfer your goal and the surplus of Vital Energy to your Higher Self. As you say aloud your manifestation goal, and with a simple act of your will—like you are giving something of value to someone—mentally send your Higher Self the extra vital energy you generated. If there is a single mental image that conveys your goal, then bring it to mind as if you were showing someone a photograph.

6. Give thanks. Even though your Higher Self does not have the kind of ego that needs to be thanked, for your own sake it is a good idea to thank it for its help. You can say something like this: "I thank you, my Higher Self, and I trust that if my goal is in alignment with you that it will be made physically manifest in your timing, and in ways I cannot even fathom. I now release this goal to your hands and end this time of meditation. So be it."

7. *Repeat daily all the steps, one through six, for seven days or more.* There is no fixed rule about how often you should repeat the procedure. Experience has taught me to apply the steps for at least three to seven consecutive days. *Important: Your goal statement and its mental picture must be absolutely the same every time you perform the steps. That way, you won't have to start over again.*

The Manifestation Revelation—the Ultimate Alignment Strategy

THIS FINAL STRATEGY IS THE most effective of all. You might wonder why I have not listed it with the other strategies. It's because it is beyond your control to initiate. It is up to your Higher Self. Let me explain what I mean.

I recently encountered a woman at an antique store who told me she had been healed from Parkinson's disease after attending a religious service. As she told me this deeply personal and lovely story, I found myself welling up with tears. It reminded me of my father's brain cancer, and all my friends who had challenges they couldn't cure.

I did not doubt her experience for a second. But at one point, she said that to truly receive the healing she had to finally give up control of her life and give it over to her Higher Power. At that point I said something reflexively, "You were never in control to begin with." With that, she looked at me quizzically but ignored my comment and kept talking. She didn't want to deal with what I meant, preferring to share more about her healing process instead. That was fine with me, of course.

However, if there is anything, and I mean *anything* I have come to accept it is this: any belief that you have personal control over your manifestations and how it ultimate affects your life is an illusion. *Your Higher Self is already in full control* over your life, your growth, your destiny and even what you manifest—even when it appears "bad."

> *The idea that we must give up control to*
> *align with our Higher Self is inaccurate*
> *and misleading. We cannot give up*
> *what we never had in the first place.*
> *All we can do is to let go of our*
> *delusion of conscious control.*

When we finally realize the truth of how the Higher Self is in full control, we can start to overcome the delusion that we are separate and apart from it, from the Divine, from each other and from anything or anyone in the Universe. We then begin to automatically align ourselves with that One Power, which was, is and shall always be ours, because it is really the power of our True Self.

> *This is what I call the manifestation*
> *revelation, and it is the best strategy*
> *for alignment with the Higher Self.*
> *It empowers us to manifest with*
> *greater awareness and a sense of*
> *purpose and peace.*

In the end, all we lack is spiritual maturity. But just as a child or a teenager has no conscious control over their physical growth, neither do we have any control over our spiritual growth. Yes, even that is up to the Higher Self.

This in no way diminishes the role of the conscious mind in our development. As the manifestation revelation dawns on us, we start to participate in our own development.

We can become as receptive as possible to the direction and guidance of the Higher Self so that we can grow as quickly as possible. That way, increasingly our manifestations will become harmonious, beautiful and bring true happiness to ourselves and others.

Give it some thought, and let the manifestation revelation come to you when you are ready. However, whether you are open to this or not, your Higher Self is busy guiding you ever onward toward change and growth.

Here is an example. When I was in my teens and early twenties, I wanted to become a professional Christian rock artist. I prayed about it, set my hopes on it, had music demos made in Nashville and even produced a music video in Los Angeles. I was serious. But within one year everything changed. My father got sick and died of brain cancer. And not only did I lose my beloved dad, I lost the one person who really believed in my music and supported my dream. When he died, I had to get a "grunt" job in the television industry and get back to reality. My Christian rock dreams faded and died, and I was left devastated.

Things turned around though. Within another year, I was in love, acquired new friends, and my spiritual beliefs had radically transformed. I no longer cared about being a Christian music recording artist because I had new, important goals.

I am glad the Universe did not grant me those musical aspirations because I might never have heard about my Higher Self. I might not have become an author to share what I have learned. I might have missed all the amazing friendships I have cherished because of this path.

It is my sincerest hope that you will use the strategies in this book to better align with your Higher Self. Further, even though you may encounter setbacks as you manifest your desires I hope you remember that your Higher Self is on your side and wants the best for you. And as you grow in your awareness, you will choose to grip less tightly to what you think your life "ought to be." Instead, you will be at peace knowing how your Higher Self is guiding you to manifest a rich and satisfying life. It is with you every step of the way.

I can think of no greater revelation than that.

About the Author

Forbes Robbins Blair is a long-time student and practitioner of all things metaphysical which includes manifestation and the Higher Self.

Mr. Blair considers it a privilege to share what he knows about manifestation with his readers and students.

Visit his website here:
http://www.forbesrobbinsblair.com

Contact him by email here:
webmaster@forbesrobbinsblair.com

Books and Products

* The Manifestation Manifesto: Amazing Technique and Strategies to Attract the Life You Want—No Visualization Required - The first book in Forbes Robbins Blair's Amazing Manifestation Strategy series, it is loaded with over 20 manifestation techniques. *Manifesto* emphasizes how to attract what you want and repel negativity. See why this book became an Amazon bestseller. Here is the link:

https://www.amazon.com/Manifestation-Manifesto-Techniques-Strategies-Visualization-ebook/dp/B00LY7ZBQG

* The Manifestation Matrix: Nine Steps to Manifest Money, Success and Love When Asking and Believing Are Not Working - The second in the Amazing Manifestation Strategies series, this book provides an easy, powerful

systematic formula for manifesting whatever you want. Its clear and practical steps only take about an hour to complete, so you can put this manifestation system to work right away. Here is the link:

http://www.amazon.com/Manifestation-Matrix-Manifest-Believing-Strategies-ebook/dp/B00UB49HBS

* The Manifestation Mindset: How to Think Like A True Manifestor and Overcome the Doubts Blocking Your Success - Is doubt blocking you from manifesting the life you want? Whether you are trying to attract money, a life partner or abundant health, this third book in the Amazing Manifestation Strategies series reveals nine ways to transform from a mere dabbler into a true manifestor. About three weeks is all it takes to see a radical shift in your thoughts and behavior, and you will be transformed into a manifestation powerhouse! Here is the link:

https://www.amazon.com/Manifestation-Mindset-Manifestor-Overcome-Strategies/dp/1522795421

* The Genie Within: Your Wish is Granted - Based on classes Mr. Blair taught in the Baltimore-Washington DC area, this eBook and Mp3 audio course teaches you how to use your creative imagination to manifest your wishes.

And it is fun, innovative, and easy to do. Here is the link:

http://www.forbesrobbinsblair.com/geniewithi n.html

* Attract Surplus Money Mp3 - This high-quality self-hypnosis audio is based on a script from the book *More Instant Self Hypnosis*. This bestselling hypnotic audio Mp3 programs your mind to attract more money. Soothing and effective, you can download and listen to it right now. Here is the link for the mp3:

http://www.forbesrobbinsblair.com/store/p17/ Attract_Wealth_hypnosis_mp3.html

* Positive Living Store – Forbes Robbins Blair's online store includes all his original products including courses, eBooks, and audio mp3s which are not for sale anywhere else. You can get more

explanation by going to his online store. Here is the link to his store:

http://www.forbesrobbinsblair.com/store/c1/F eatured_Products.html

* Soul of the Knight: Awaken the Warrior Within - Tap into your inner confidence, discipline, and motivation as you connect with the noble Knight within. This eBook/audio Mp3 program is like nothing else. If you are drawn to the image of medieval Knights, this program can help you transform your life quickly and dramatically. Mr. Blair believes it is the most powerful product he has ever produced. Download it today. Here is the link:

http://www.forbesrobbinsblair.com/_soul-of-the-knight.html

* Instant Self Hypnosis: How to Hypnotize Yourself with Your Eyes Open - Stop smoking, lose weight, and stop stressing out. In his original bestselling book, Forbes Robbins Blair reveals his remarkable method that allows you to hypnotize yourself as you read. This bestselling international classic contains 35 powerful scripts to improve your life in practical ways. You will use this book repeatedly. Here is the link: http://www.amazon.com/Instant-Self-Hypnosis-Hypnotize-Yourself-Your-ebook/dp/B00348UMQM

* Self Hypnosis Revolution: The Amazingly Simple Way to Use Self Hypnosis to Change Your Life - Learn how everyday tasks like taking out the garbage can be used with the power of suggestion to create remarkable transformations in five key areas of your life. This innovative autosuggestion method is easy, fun and takes no extra time out of your day. Here is the link:

http://www.amazon.com/Self-Hypnosis-Revolution-Amazingly-Simple-Change/dp/1402206704

* More Instant Self Hypnosis: Hypnotize Yourself as You Read - The sequel to *Instant Self Hypnosis*, this book contains 48 more self-improvement scripts covering a wide variety of topics such as "Achieve Your Potential" and "Feel More Sexy." Includes Master Induction 2.0, an improvement on the original. There are also interactive experiments to help you understand self-hypnosis better and prepare you to hypnotize

yourself as you read. Just read to succeed. Here is the link:

https://www.amazon.com/MORE-Instant-Self-Hypnosis-Hypnotize-ebook/dp/B003V1WIIC

<u>* Self Hypnosis As You Read: 42 Life Changing Scripts</u> – Includes the scripts: "Lose the Last 10 Pounds," "Never Be Late Again," "Save More Money." These are just a few of the hypnosis script titles in this book, based on the most requested topics of the readers and fans of *Instant Self Hypnosis*. This book contains multiple scripts to induce hypnosis with the eyes-open method, as well as advanced material never published before. Some readers say it is

Mr. Blair's best self-hypnosis work. Here is the link: http://www.amazon.com/Self-Hypnosis-As-You-Read-ebook/dp/B00FRK2Y4S

Thank You

Thank you for taking the time to read *The Manifestation Revelation.* I am fortunate and honored to share with you these strategies about the Higher Self and its relationship to manifestation.

If you enjoyed this book, would you do me a favor and write a customer review at amazon.com? Just tell people what you liked about it. Your opinion really makes a difference.

Happy Manifesting!

Notes

Made in the USA
Monee, IL
13 June 2023